PAXTON STREET

LEONTYNE CLAY PECK

Copyright 2002
All rights reserved. No part of this book may be reproduced, stored in a retrieval system or transmitted in any form or by any means, electronic, mechanical, photocopy, or otherwise, without permission in writing from the author.
Inquiries should be forwarded to: leontynepeck@gmail.com

ISBN 0-9740920-3-7

Library of Congress Copyright
Book Design by Leontyne Clay Peck
Self Published by Leontyne Clay Peck
Printed by Lulu Publishing-Raleigh, NC

Dedication

This book is dedicated to memories of my sisters, Cynthia Clay Stradwick and Llwendolyn Clay and to the memory of my college friend, Simi L. Hicks.

PAXTON STREET STORIES

The Grapevine

Miss Marthie

1953

Suzy Q

Paper & Linoleum

Miss Laura

Ring Ring Ring

Johnny Walker Red Christmas

Venison

Ginny Whistle

Vomit

Starving Spirits

Nash Rambler

Thea Garland-Girl Extraordinaire

Paris

Miss Mabel's Custard

Nink

The Majestic Theatre

Dear Whitney and Alexis and my future grandchildren,

This book of vignettes is a stroll down memory lane for me. I hope that it will be inspirational to you both now and in the future. Don't be afraid to live your lives, make mistakes, take risks and enjoy each day that the Almighty has given to you. These are my memories. Some of the stories were difficult to write. The content is not written to hurt anyone, but instead to encourage. Life is difficult for most of us, yet we can triumph over life's challenges.

Paxton Street is a collection of stories from my childhood. I would like to share with others who may want to laugh, cry and be inspired by these stories.

As you make your way through this maze called life always remember that many of the paths that you will take, I have already navigated. I am familiar with the terrain. It is possible that you may never travel down some of those same roads.

I know that you will fall and stumble into some of the potholes, just as I did. The important thing is not that you stumbled, but that you get back up and keep moving. There will be days that you will absolutely not feel like getting up again. The Almighty will always be there to help you up when you fall.

Living on Paxton Street was a wonderful experience for me. I only wish that the rest of my life had been as enjoyable. There were many wonderful people in my neighborhood that nurtured me during my youth. It was another place in time. The lessons that I learned will stay with me forever.

Love,
Mom

804 Buckingham Road, Cumberland, Maryland

"The Grapevine"

1967

The purple, sweet, round goblets of fruit called my name every day as I walked by the Paxton House. They whispered, "Gaye, come over and pluck us from the vines. You won't get in trouble. Your Grandma Laura will never find out." The whispers became shouts as they enticed me to come closer.

I tried to avoid the sidewalk by walking in the middle of the street. I did not want to yield to the temptation. Mrs. Paxton's six-foot wood fence could not adequately protect the vines from my tiny, brown fingers.

The temptation to grab a handful of those grapes overwhelmed me. Every day the aroma of the grapes blew in the breeze. I made it my mission to taste them. I don't know if anyone ever saw me "steal" the grapes and I didn't care.

I was eight years old. I didn't have many luxuries in my life. Mrs. Paxton's grapes were the highlight of my day. On my way home from school, I made a special trip to the Paxton Grape Vines.

Mrs. Paxton probably saw me take her grapes. I know that her housekeeper, Miss Marthie Washington, saw me stealing the grapes. Mrs. Paxton was a white lady who lived on Paxton Street. The street was named for her husband's family.

My neighborhood was called Back Street. The neighborhood consisted of two dusty little streets, Paxton and Water. The vibrant neighborhood consisted primarily of African American families. Most of the families were poor. We didn't know that we were poor so we really enjoyed our lives. We shared good and bad times. Love and Laughter were always present in our little, dusty "hood."

The Paxton Family was one of the few white families remaining in our neighborhood. Their large, red, brick home was pretty. It stood prominently on the corner of Paxton & Water Streets. I remember the day that their daughter, Connie got married. I don't know if any black people attended the wedding. I do know that when she and her new husband departed for their honeymoon; we all sat on our porches to bid her farewell.

That particular event sticks in my mind because it seemed that when Connie moved, others (black and white) began to move too. They moved into other Piedmont neighborhoods. Some even moved to our rival city of Keyser.

The 1960s were beginning to be ushered out and the sweeping changes of the 1970s were about to significantly change Back Street. My dad said that he would never leave Back Street. He kept his word until 1990 when a fire destroyed his home and he had to move. He and my mother purchased a home outside of Keyser, West Virginia.

The Paxton Family moved out of the neighborhood. As the years went by, other families moved in and out of the stately Paxton House. The house began to deteriorate and the grapes lost their flavor. Once the Paxton's moved, I never went back to the vines – they simply weren't the same.

The expression, "I heard it through the grapevine," is so appropriate for Back Street. We had real grapevines. Although the grapevines are gone, the community never lost her sweet and affectionate network of Back Street citizens.

Miss Marthie

Miss Martha Washington was a petite, "firecracker" of a woman. She was small, but mighty. "Miss Marthie," as she was affectionately known in our community, was our neighbor. Martha Louise Washington was born on June 11, 1904 in Paw Paw, West Virginia. She did days work for the Paxton Family. She was also the wet nurse for the Paxton children. She knew all the gossip in the African American community, as well as the white community.

I have never met anyone quite as colorful, humorous, industrious and smart as Miss Marthie. I loved her and her family. Miss Marthie was one of the few "colored" people in town who owned her own home. Her home was always immaculate.

This feisty woman was a devoted mother. All of her children graduated from high school, which was quite an accomplishment for black students during the 1940s and 1950s. She was an entrepreneur. She had two unique talents. She could iron clothing; especially white shirts, better than any professional service. She had a loyal clientele from the "tri-townies."

Before permanent press clothing became popular, Miss Marthie was our community's secret weapon against wrinkles. She had a special technique that only she knew. My mom relied heavily on Miss Marthie to iron many of our "rags" as she referred to our clothing.

Cigarette smoking is taboo now and potentially deadly, but many of the women in our community, including Miss Marthie were smokers. She smoked unfiltered cigarettes. She had the ability to hold the cigarette in the clutches of her bottom lip.

The cigarette never fell out of her mouth. The ashes continued to grow as the cigarette burned. Sometimes the ashes were longer than the cigarette and they never fell. She had control of that cigarette! I used to watch in amazement how the ashes grew. I often thought to myself that Miss Marthie was going to burn her lips. I don't think that she ever did.

My mother is an excellent cook. Often she would run out of key ingredients to complete the recipe. We knew that if we ran out of anything, we could always go to Miss Marthie and borrow it. Miss Marthie's tiny kitchen was always swirling with activity. Rochelle, one of her granddaughters was frying potatoes and onions. Her son, Dickie was filling the silver, tin cooler with ice and beer and her beau, Mr. Stanley was sipping a cup of black coffee.

Miss Marthie's oldest daughter, Izetta (nicknamed Babe), sat comfortably in her oversized chair. Babe had suffered a stroke. Her mind was sharp as a tack, but her physical body was impaired. As a result of the stroke, she often drifted in and out of sleep. When her snoring became louder than a locomotive; Miss Marthie would shake her and say, "Babe, wake up!" Babe would immediately wake up and resume whatever she was doing, which was typically watching the afternoon soap operas.

Miss Marthie stood at the ironing board pressing a crisp, white shirt. I loved going to Miss Marthie's house! She had a white, metal cupboard filled with seasonings and food. My mother would dispatch me to Miss Marthie's house to borrow sugar, salt, pepper, paprika, laundry detergent, and cigarettes. You name it. We borrowed it.

Miss Marthie always started her sentences with the word "for." One day, I visited Miss Marthie's home about five or six times to borrow one thing or another. After my last visit, I remember her turning to me and saying in a comical manner, "for, Gaye, tell your mother that this is not the Five and Dime Store." I laughed uncontrollably. It was clear to me that we depended upon the goodness of Miss Marthie to supplement our cupboard. I think her cupboard served as the unofficial neighborhood "store." In our neighborhood, we all shared from our cupboards.

The back of our house was situated about twenty feet from the back of Miss Marthie's house. Our homes were so close together that we could actually engage in conversations while gazing out our windows. I wouldn't want to live that close to anyone now. It was fun during that time.

In the 1970s, it was common for the ladies in the community to have laundry day. I always hated laundry day. I knew that along with laundry day came soup beans and cornbread for dinner. I hated soup beans. I loved cornbread with melted butter and grape jelly. Now, I like soup beans but I didn't when I was kid. My younger brother, "Beaver," was a cute little boy. He had bright, brown eyes, a dimple in his cheek and a jack-o-lantern smile. He also had a reputation of being a mischievous boy.

Beaver along with his buddies would tease Miss Marthie. These mini African warriors were simply boys engaging in G.I. Joe combat. Miss Marthie and Miss See (another neighbor) were unknowingly in the combat zone of the Beaver Brigade. Poor Miss Marthie and Miss See had no idea that their own backyards had been designated as enemy territory.

One warm spring day, Miss Marthie was hanging her clothes on the clothesline. The warm breeze of the wind lyrically swung the garments back and forth. The fresh linen smell mingled with the aromatic spring air.

My mother was looking out the window of our house. She noticed that Miss Marthie was tugging at the bottom of her blue skirt. It seemed as though something was agitating her. She kept swatting at something and then all of a sudden she let out a loud cry. Mom rushed out of the house to see what was wrong.

"For something has stung me in the butt! The bees must be bad this year," She shouted. "Miss Marthie, I don't see any bees." My mom said. "Well, something was sure stinging me. It had to be bees!" Miss Marthie adamantly stated. Mom assisted Miss Marthie into her house. On the way towards the house, she noticed some bbs on the ground.

She started to laugh under her breath. She knew that the bees hadn't stung Miss Marthie. The "bees" were the pellets from Beaver's bb gun. Beaver and his buddies were hiding in the bushes shooting at Miss Marthie's derriere. Her yard had been designated as enemy territory for that spring day.

1953

My oldest sister, Cindi, was born on August 11, 1953 in Keyser, West Virginia at Potomac Valley Hospital. She was the first child born to our mother. Cindi was five years my senior. She assumed the big sister role very well. In many ways she had maturity beyond her years. Cindi was pretty. Her complexion was considered "high yellow." She had big, beautiful, blue eyes. Our grandma, Mabel, also had beautiful blue eyes.

Cindi's fingernails were her trademark. She had pretty hands and her nails were always polished with outrageous colors. Indeed, her nails looked artificial. One of the things that Cindi used to do for me was give me her discarded nails. I know that sounds disgusting. I was a kid all of about six years old. I had short stubby nails. Once her nails reached a certain length, she would clip the top portion of the nails off and give them to me. I would then put glue on the nails and attach them to my nails. Voila! Instant nails that lasted for about a day. It was so much fun. I think Cindi got a kick out of me wanting her nails.

I was the "little" sister. Cindi also considered me the tattletale. Cindi and some of her teen friends would chase boys, hang out at Charlie Johnson's store, smoke cigarettes and go for joy rides in cars. In order to keep an "extra" eye on Cindi, my mom would make Cindi watch me, which meant that I had to tag along. Cindi hated when I tagged along with her because she knew that I would blab about everything she did. She would even try to bribe me with huge bags of candy. Once I got the candy, I promised Cindi that I wouldn't tell mom that she had been smoking or getting into cars with boys.

I really intended to keep my promise. Once we returned home from our adventure, mom would interrogate me. I always blurted out the truth. I really wanted to remain silent and not tell on Cindi. Mom always won. I broke my promise to Cindi every time. Cindi would get punished and the "little tattle tale" would get an ice cream reward from mom. Our small, white house in Keyser did not have indoor plumbing. We had an outhouse located in the lower portion of our backyard. After a period of time Cindi became weary of my tattling. She began to engage me in her cigarette smoking habit. I was six years old.

Cindi started smoking cigarettes at the young age of eleven. As a matter of fact, many kids in our Virginia Street neighborhood were smokers. It was the cool thing to do. Both of our parents smoked, but they did not want us to smoke. Unfortunately, Cindi's smoking became addictive and she endured many punishments because of her smoking. Her smoking was not a behavior problem, but an addiction problem.

The outhouse served as Cindi's private smoking headquarters. Each time that Cindi went to the outhouse to smoke, she would take me with her. She would make me take a "puff." I hated cigarettes then and I do now. She told me that I could not tell on her for smoking because I was also smoking. I never told on her. I didn't know that this was a form of blackmail, but then again I was only about six years old.

One day, Cindi, Susie Hott, and I were "smoking" in the outhouse. Unexpectedly, daddy came and flung the door open on the outhouse and caught us. He sent Susie home to her parents. He spanked and punished Cindi and me. I had two older sisters. Cindi was my older sister. We had a middle sister named Llwendolyn. She died in infancy. My mother once told me that she was going to nickname us Cindy, Lindy and Windy. I was going to be called Lindy—Lindy Clay!

A turning point happened in my family that forever changed my relationship with my sister. Our parents divorced. My siblings and I moved to Piedmont to live with our paternal grandmother, Laura. I was about seven years old. I had just finished the First Grade at Keyser Elementary School. Cindi was 12 years old. They were very tough years for our entire family, but because of God's grace, mercy and love we endured.

My sister and I bonded during those years. She became maternal towards our brothers and me. She loved and protected us. She and I fought and disagreed about many things over the years. Our personalities were very different, but she taught me many lessons about life.

Christmas had always been an enjoyable time for me. I can't recall ever having a bad Christmas. There was always plenty of food, toys, decorations and neighborhood gatherings. Even when our mother did not live with us, she would come and visit us for Christmas. She and my dad would always manage to fight sometime during the holiday, but never on Christmas Day.

The Christmas of 1967 was a memorable one for me. Cindi took me shopping in Downtown Keyser. Daddy had given her money to buy gifts for us. Navy "P" Coats were popular. Cindi purchased a blue one, and a little, matching one for me. I felt grown up because I was dressed like my sister. I have held on to that memory of my sister all of my life because it warms the depths of my heart. In 2000, the "P" Coats made a fashion return. I purchased one for my youngest daughter, Alexis. It reminded me of that special day in 1967.

My sister was with me through the good times and the bad. She was there when I smoked my first cigarette, got my first bra, attended my first dance at the Piedmont Legion, purchased hot pants and platform shoes, had child dental surgery at Potomac Valley Hospital, graduated from college, gave birth to my children, and married my husband. My sister was with me for every significant event in my life.

Those years of smoking finally caught up with my Cindi. We used to fight all the time about her "bad" habit. I told her that smoking would be the death of her. During the 1980s, we shared an apartment together in Silver Spring, Maryland. The only place that she was allowed to smoke in the apartment was in her bedroom. I really tried to encourage her to stop smoking. She honestly tried several times. She just couldn't quit. The addiction was a strangling one.

She knew that smoking would probably kill her. The years of smoking ravaged her lungs. The last time that I saw my sister she was in hospice. We drank champagne, ate some snacks, shared warm memories and laughed. We celebrated the New Year. She departed on January 4, 1994.

SUZY Q

A small playground was situated near my grandparent's modest home in Petersburg, WV. It was originally the colored children's playground. This playground was where my brother, "Beaver" and our friends, P.A. and Russy (or Suzy Q as she was called by her Grandma Lil) developed our theatrical skills.

Russy and P.A. were siblings. Russy's real name is Lillian Russell hence the nickname Russy. A true West Virginian has a nickname or two. P.A.'s given name is Percy Adolphus. He looked like a movie star. He could have been the leading man in any Hollywood movie.

Our favorite thing to do was to pretend to be movie stars. I loved Dorothy Dandridge, so I pretended to be her. I used my sample Avon lipsticks for my makeup and I wrapped a towel around my head as a turban, just like the movie stars.

Each day our little group met at the old school house for rehearsal. The schoolhouse was situated practically in my grandmother's yard. Naturally, I was always in charge of the production. P.A. loved Elvis Presley, thus he always was our Elvis impersonator (a very good one, I might add). Russy was the beauty queen, so she had to learn her special wave and wear a crown that we created from construction paper. Beaver pretended to be either James Brown or one of his own made up characters. He had a cape that was also used as a bathrobe.

We sang and danced all day, just the four of us. Occasionally, my cousin Angel would join our performance. She thought that her job was to be our boss. Most days she succeeded at this task. Angel had beautiful, long, black braids. She looked like an angel but behaved more like a devil. Although she was extremely mischievous, she was full of fun. My other cousin, Gordy would occasionally join us. Angel and Gordy had a love/hate relationship. She loved to boss him and he hated it! We had great fun playing games, swinging on the swings and swirling on the merry-go-round.

We didn't have streetlights in our area so we had to go home as soon as the darkness emerged. It was really scary at night. Sometimes we sat on the porch and Grandpap Pid told us ghost stories. I have fond memories of my summers in Petersburg, West Virginia.

PAPER & LINOLEUM

Did your mother put newspaper down on the floor to keep it clean? I think just about every house in Piedmont had newspaper on top of the floor (to keep it clean). Rarely did we see the beautiful patterns of our floors because they were always covered with the obituary pages from the Piedmont Herald, the Cumberland Times or the Keyser News Tribune! I could catch up on a week's worth of news just by "reading" our floor.

I hated newspaper on the floor. I swore that when I grew up, I would never, ever put newspaper on the floor. The paper would make a crunchy noise when you walked on top of it. They wouldn't stay down on the floor, so you were constantly organizing them to keep them looking neat. Those newspapers drove me crazy. You couldn't escape them in our neighborhood. It was almost as though; all the women in the community had sworn an oath of cleanliness by using this dirt catcher technique.

One spring day after mom had finished scrubbing the kitchen floor at our home at 42 Water Street. I approached her and ask her why she had to put the "cover" over the floor. I told her that I thought it was stupid to cover the floor with newspaper. It just didn't make any sense to me. The floor is a walking surface not a recycling center.

I didn't know what to expect from her response. I was hoping that she would say that she would stop this insane custom. Instead, I got a lecture from her on housekeeping tips. She looked straight into my eyes with her piercing green eyes and said, "Gayedy, when you have your own house, you can clean it the way you want. This is my house and I'll clean it the way I see fit.

This Piedmont dirt is the blackest, nastiest dirt that God ever made. I'm not breaking my back scrubbing this damn floor every day. That's why I put newspaper on the floor. It will stay clean at least for a few days. When you become a mother, you'll understand what I'm talking about." She made it clear that she didn't like the newspapers on the floor either. Until a better solution was found to keep the floor clean, she was in no hurry to cancel her newspaper subscription.

It was not about the newspapers for her, but about her solutions in maintaining a clean home. We lived in a total of two houses on Paxton Street and three houses on Water Street. Mom continued to put newspaper on her floors in every one of our homes. I believe that she discontinued her practice when she moved from Piedmont to New Creek nine years ago. So, I guess it was that Piedmont dirt after all.

Miss Laura

The black Cadillac pulled up in front of 23 Paxton Street. The white lady sitting inside the vehicle pressed her hand gently against the horn and tooted. Grandma Laura quickly finished her tea and cinnamon toast. She softly shouted, "It's Miss Vi, I'm leaving now. I'll see you later today." Laura gathered her purse and quietly slipped out of the house.

I was home that day sick from school with a toothache. Unfortunately, I inherited soft teeth from both sides of my family and my teeth were prone to decay. I frequently had toothaches. I was snuggled under warm blankets in Grandma Laura's bed because I spent the night in her bed so that she could cuddle me and soothe my pain. Grandma always knew what to do. She had all kinds of concoctions that she would mix together to ease pain. She even put whiskey on my swollen gums to help with the pain. It worked because it knocked me out.

Grandma was an early riser. I slept under the protection of her warm body all night. When she got up to get ready to go to work, I missed her warmth. She worked as a domestic. I woke up as soon as she moved her petite, golden body. I gazed at her, as she got ready for the day. She would make sure that everyone was settled, before she left the house. She had many people to look after. She and Grandpap Willie had a houseful of people living with them. In total, there were seven adults and eight children who resided in Grandma's four-bedroom home.

Grandma's philosophy in life was that her babies (grand, great grand, great great grand etc.) were hers and none of her babies would ever go hungry or homeless; she didn't care what she had to do to take care of them. She was a hardworking, honest and sweet woman.

She and my dad had a strong mother/son bond. He was the third of her four sons. My dad had come home from working last shift at the local paper mill. Grandma thought that I was asleep and couldn't hear her conversation with daddy. I could hear the two of them talking. They were sitting at the tiny kitchen table drinking coffee. The kitchen was situated beside Grandma's bedroom.

I could hear their conversation. "Russell, we need to do something about Gaye's toothaches. They are starting to get worse. I feel so sorry for her. She was up all night crying. I want you to call Dr. Fanti and arrange for him to extract those teeth. I don't care what it takes, that baby can't take that pain anymore." I couldn't hear daddy's response. All I know is that very shortly after that conversation, I was admitted to Potomac Valley Hospital to have those miserable teeth extracted. Halleuyah!

Grandma liked to can vegetables and fruits. She also loved to make homemade root beer. She and my Aunt Chrissy baked the most delicious pies and cakes. On Saturday afternoons, Grandma would work in her kitchen preparing food for the traditional Sunday Soul Food (after church) dinner. One of the things that we could always count on for dessert was Grandma's famous caramel cake. The cake and icing were made from scratch. It was mouth watering. I can taste it now.

Perhaps what I remember most about Grandma's kitchen is that she allowed us (her grandkids) in the kitchen with her while she was doing the cooking. Grandma loved having us in the kitchen with her. She provided miniature baking pans and utensils for us. When she baked her cakes and pies; we baked our *little* cakes and pies. It was the best time of my life.

My grandmother was the housekeeper for several ladies who lived in the neighboring community of Westernport, Maryland. I never could figure out why these ladies could not clean their own homes. After all, they were home all day. What were they doing all day that they couldn't clean their own homes?

Later in life, I learned that having a black housekeeper was a status symbol for white women. In many ways it still is today. I know many women who don't work outside the home and have a housekeeper. Explain that to me, because I don't get it. I wish that I had it so easy. I work in, out, around, beneath, and on top of my house and believe me it is exhausting. I can only imagine the fatigue of my grandmother and her contemporaries.

Grandma had to clean their homes; then come home and take care of her family and home. She did it with a smile and wonderful grace. Fortunately many of the ladies who employed Grandma were very kind to her.

My first Barbie, Midge, Scooter, Pepper, Allen and Ken dolls came from one of the little girls that grandma used to baby-sit. I played with those dolls until I was about 11 years old. I built my Barbies a house out of a large refrigerator box. We couldn't afford the Barbie Dream house, so I improvised. Grandma gave me some of her scrap materials for the curtains and carpeting.

The exterior of the house was "painted" with crayons. The great thing about my Barbie house was that I was able to also fit inside of the house. I got inside of that box and played for hours with my dolls. I even made them cars out of old shoeboxes.

I kept my dolls until I went away to college. Daddy stored them in the cellar at 37 Water Street. One fateful day in 1979, my dad decided to clean out all of the old toys that were stored in the cellar. Guess what? He threw all my Barbie memorabilia away.

I had the original Barbie with the Black & White Swimsuit. In an instant, Barbie, Ken, Allen, Midge, Scooter and Pepper were gone forever and taken away to the city dump. I was devastated. It didn't make matters any better when daddy said that he also threw away

Beaver's G.I. Joe. To this day, I don't know why daddy threw our stuff away. I guess he just got tired of storing it.

Arthritis was a formidable challenger for Grandma. Her petite, brown hands were virtually closed because of crippling rheumatoid arthritis. I don't know how she managed to knead bread; braid hair, sweep and other manual tasks with her fragile hands. It was amazing all the things that she accomplished. She had a strong will and a deep faith in the Almighty.

My grandmother was a blessing to her family and her community. I often can't imagine where I would be without her love and support. I know that I'm a better person because of her influence upon my life.

Ring…Ring…Ring….
Telephonus Disconnectus

I was thrilled when the monopolistic telephone company was broken up into little baby bells. I grew up during the time when the telephone company would not hesitate to disconnect your service. They didn't care what your circumstances were. They would not allow the customers to make payment arrangements. If your service was disconnected, you had to pay a hefty deposit, plus the bill to get service restored. The odds were if you don't have the money to pay the bill; you certainly didn't have the money to pay a security deposit.

In the 1960s, the telephone was considered a luxury. In our community, neighbors often shared telephones. Our family always had a telephone, because my mother loved to talk on the phone. Unfortunately mom suffered from "telephoneitis." She could not control her long distance calling. As a result of her phone addiction, our telephone was frequently disconnected. The bills were astronomical and my dad simply refused to pay. Generally once your phone was connected, it stayed disconnected for months.

Miss Marthie always came to the rescue whenever our phone was disconnected. She would let us use her phone. I never remember her phone being disconnected. Her living room sometimes seemed like Grand Central Station. There were always people in her house waiting to receive or make a call. Can you imagine today with all the technology that we have, waiting to make a telephone call? One thing is for certain; today's consumers have many more telecommunications choices. In the words of Lily Tomlin's telephone operator character, Ernestine, "One ringie dingie, two ringie dingie."

Johnny Walker Red

The warm ambience of the room was inviting. Tall, beautiful candles adorned the tops of the glass tables. The living room was cozy, the softness of the glow of the candles created an aura of solitude. The jazz of John Coltrane played on the stereo.

I can't remember the whereabouts of my family that particular evening. All I remember is that mom and I were home alone. My dad was probably at work. Rusty, my older brother lived with my maternal grandparents in Petersburg, WV. He wanted to play football in high school and Piedmont High School did not have a football program. Rusty moved to Petersburg to live with our grandparents to attend school. My sister, Cindi, was living in Wheeling, WV. Beaver was probably at the neighbor's house playing with his buddies Jeff and Tyrone.

My mother always loved to entertain, much to the chagrin of my dad. We always had company in our home. It was like a hotel; sometimes there were people in my house that I didn't even know. Our house was identified as the party house. If you wanted to party – 37 Water Street was the place to be. Everyone was welcome.

Sue Clay had a reputation for having good food and good liquor at her parties. However, only her closest friends got to drink her Johnny Walker Red Scotch. Her preferred libation was Scotch and only Johnny Walker would satisfy her taste. She had card parties, pig feet parties, cookouts, birthday parties, funeral parties, motorcycle gang parties, 373 baseball parties – any occasion was a cause for celebration.

A quiet home was an anomaly for me. Whenever the house was quiet that meant that someone was either sick or dead. I was kind of nervous when I saw my mom being quiet; it was so contrary to her nature. I guess that everyone needs quiet time.

Our stereo was not your average run of the mill stereo. It was a master blaster of a stereo. It was a 6-foot long wood console. It was so long that it actually looked like a coffin. The front façade of the console had decorative, red velvet material sewn onto four wood panels. The wood panels were moveable and could slide across the front of the stereo.

Another lovely feature were the blinking lights built inside the system directly behind the speakers. The velvet speaker covers were designed to slide from side to side and to expose the blinking lights. The blinking of the lights coordinated with the tempo of the music. I guess that was to simulate the disco effect.

If Barry White's songs were playing, the lights would blink slowly. If the Jackson Five were playing; the lights danced in all different directions. The most awesome feature was the 8-track disc player built into the system. That stereo had it's own personality. It played constantly, from morning until night.

"Miss Velveteen," the stereo's nickname would guide her spindle and arm against the black grooves of the albums that held the tunes of Aretha Franklin, Sarah Vaughn, Nancy Wilson, Jimmy Smith, Nina Simone, Junior Walker, John Coltrane and our cousin, Don Redman.

Mom was in the living room sitting on the sofa. I was sitting at the kitchen table painting my fingernails. Our living room and kitchen were adjoining so mom and I could see each other. I could look from the kitchen into the living room. We had a big picture window in our living room.

Gazing through the picture window, I could see the beautiful, soft snowflakes dancing to the music of the wind. It was cold and blustery outside but it was warm inside our home. Mom sat cozily on the sofa gazing out the window. Her legs tucked underneath her body. Her Kent cigarette dangled from her rose colored lips.

In her hand, she held a small cocktail glass of Johnny Walker Red Scotch. She had all she needed for a relaxing evening – Coltrane, Johnny Walker Red and Kent Cigarettes. I guess the Piedmont V.F.W., her favorite hang out was closed that night.

VENISON
In remembrance of Rudolph

I was about five years old. I believed that Santa was going to bring me everything on my Christmas list. I especially wanted my own pearl colored vanity set, complete with stool and makeup. Daddy assured me that if I was a good girl; I would get my vanity.

Fortunately, I was a good girl most of the time. If you don't count the time when I tried to burn down our house. That's another story. If daddy had just let me stay outside and play with my friends, I probably would not have set fire to the roll of toilet paper that engulfed his bed.

After daddy set "fire" to my skinny, brown butt with his bare hand for my transgression, I never played with fire again. As a matter of fact, even to this day, when I see flames I start to feel some pain in my derriere. I knew that I could be a good girl for Santa.

Daddy said that Rudolph, the Red nosed reindeer would bring Santa to our house. Rudolph, according to Daddy, had special powers and could fly through the air. Even at five years old, I didn't believe that reindeer could fly. Many parents share this fairy tale with their children. You probably believed your parents too.

I told our neighbors, Sam and Becky, that Santa was going to bring me a vanity set. I invited them to come over on Christmas Day to see it. They said that they would definitely come over and visit us on Christmas Day. I was so excited. I couldn't wait for the special day. Mom promised that Santa would also bring a make up set to go with the vanity. I couldn't wait to smear my face with purple eye color and crimson lipstick. I always loved to play dress up. Now I was about to get some more equipment to help me.

Daddy was an avid outdoorsman. He loved the outdoors and was always busy outside doing something. The man simply never sat still, that's probably why he always remained a slender man. He and his buddies always hunted and fished in the West Virginia wilderness. Daddy routinely planned his vacation around the West Virginia Hunting Season and the West Virginia State Basketball Championship Games. Those events were very special times for him. We knew where our vacations were going to be every year and Disneyland was never in the plans.

He would do a safety inspection on his guns prior to hunting season. He taught us about gun safety. We never had a problem understanding the danger of firearms. None of us ever bothered his guns or hunting gear – it quite simply was off limits. Daddy didn't own a gun cabinet. Often his rifles were (unloaded of course) lying across his bed or underneath his bed. We knew they were there. We also knew never to go near or touch them. My father was a very loving, but strict disciplinarian. His voice commanded respect. The thought of a whipping from him kept us walking the chalk line.

There are different seasons to hunt different animals. He hunted squirrels, deer and other critters. My sister, Cindi, never ate wild meat after she became an adult. She said that she had eaten too much wild meat when she was a child and she refused to eat another morsel of wild meat.

Daddy used every part of the animal for his culinary delight. His favorite recipe was squirrel meat with gravy and toast. It was his specialty. He loved it. We hated it. He and Granny Clampett, from the Beverly Hillbillies, probably shared the same recipe.

However, we did like the Squirrel Tail Hats that he made for us. It was like a badge of honor to wear those squirrel tail hats to school. All of the kids in the community had them.

It was November and the weather was getting colder. The thoughts of Christmas coming still overwhelmed my little mind. I just kept counting down the days. I wanted Thanksgiving to come and get out of the way so that the most splendid holiday could arrive.

Daddy was preoccupied cleaning his guns. He was getting ready for hunting season. I did not understand the difference between deer and reindeer. In my mind, deer were not special. They couldn't fly like Santa's Reindeer.

Daddy left the house early in the morning to go hunting. Sometimes he stayed in the forest for hours stalking his prey. Most of the time he came home empty handed, but not this day. He hit the jackpot and landed a buck. At this point, I had never seen anything that daddy had killed. He usually skinned his animals before I had a chance to see them in their rigimortis state.

Daddy strapped his buck to the top of his car and brought him home for everyone to see. Excitement filled the house. After all, this was a hunter's accomplishment – to "bag" a buck. This was his trophy. My mother called the neighbors to come and see Russ' buck. Have you ever tasted venison? It is simply delicious if prepared properly. My mom's venison recipe was très magnifique! She made a Bar-B-Que sauce for her venison.

I was excited too. I peeked out the front room window. I was astonished at what I saw. Rudolph was strapped to the top of daddy's car. I was horrified! I started to cry. I couldn't understand it. Why had my daddy killed Rudolph the Reindeer? I thought he was going to kill the deer not Santa's Reindeer. No vanity set for me. No Christmas for anyone. Daddy had destroyed Rudolph! I couldn't stop crying.

I was too upset to go outside and join the others who were "admiring" the catch of the day. I was mad at daddy. I was going to ask him why he killed Rudolph. About thirty minutes passed and the neighbors slowly began to go home. Daddy came into the house and he saw that I had been crying. He looked at me and said, "What's the matter with you, why are you crying?" "You killed Rudolph and now we can't have Christmas!" I blurted out.

Everyone started to laugh, especially daddy. "Baby, I didn't kill Rudolph. Remember Rudolph has a red nose and the deer that I got in the forest does not have a red nose." I became instantly happy. On Christmas Day, Sam and Becky came over to see my vanity set. Mom cooked barbeque venison, potato salad, greens, sweet potatoes, and rolls for everyone.

Ginny Whistle

"Hey, Little Ginny Whistles, how are you doing today?" Frank Stewart shouted as my little brother, Beaver and I exited from the Davis Bakery.
"We're fine" we both chimed in unison. "Tell Big Ginny Whistle that I said hello!" "O.K., we will."

Beaver and I loved Mr. Frank Stewart. We never knew much about him except that he was mom's friend. He lived in the hill section of Piedmont. We had two neighborhoods in Piedmont. We had downtown neighborhoods and Up on the Hill neighborhoods. We lived downtown.

He seemed to always be in a happy mood. He always made us laugh. He was such a nice man. He called us "Little Ginny Whistles." Mom was big Ginny Whistle. I don't ever remember Frank calling us by our given names. He was the only person in Piedmont who called us "Little Ginny Whistles." We never knew what a Ginny Whistle was. Do you? Even mom said she didn't know what a Ginny Whistle was, but it was Frank's term of endearment for us.

In Piedmont, everyone had a nickname. Some people had multiple nicknames. Typically, you didn't learn a person's legal names until upon death. My nickname was Punkin'. Only a few people in the community called me by that name. Most people called me Gaye. I liked the name Gaye; however my last name was Clay. Believe me having a rhyming name is no fun. My high school teachers, Mrs. Twigg and Mrs. Iverson, always called me Leontyne. They both insisted that I use my first name.

On the other hand, my younger brother Roderick was stuck with the nickname, Beaver. To this day everyone from our community calls him Beaver. Do you know any grown men named Beaver? I know about five men who are called Beaver. I guess it could have been worse; we could have been called Muskrat or Ginny Whistle!

VOMIT

It was 8:00 a.m. I could hear the grunting and gurgling sounds coming from the bathroom. She was doing it again, regurgitating her food. The familiar sound of vomiting became a common practice in our apartment. As I lay in my bed, I could hear the thrusting sound of liquidized food being propelled into the ceramic toilet. It was a disgusting sound. I hated to hear it. I didn't know how to stop it. To drown out the sound, I simply turned up the volume on my record player. Roy Ayer's song "You Send Me" was playing.

Simi and I decided to move off campus. We rented a two-bedroom/two bathroom apartment. The apartment was nice, but it was too far from campus. We had to get up very early in the morning to drive to school. We both had cars, but the thirty-minute commute during rush hour was extremely unpleasant. Our apartment was located in Southeast Washington, quite a distant from the ritzy American University neighborhood.

We moved to our apartment in Southeast D.C. We couldn't afford the apartments located near the campus. We really should have kept our butts on campus. We were immature. We thought that we were prepared for adult responsibilities.

Simi was so much fun. She had a great sense of humor. She was extremely generous, sometimes to a fault. Her physique was quite imposing and intimidating. She stood over six feet tall and weighed over 250 pounds. Her skin was dark, smooth and like satin. She said her secret for beautiful skin was Johnson's baby products. She used Johnson's baby products on her body and face everyday.

Her upper torso was small. She complained about not having any boobs. She had big hips (like a lot of sisters). She had, what I called, a New York sense of fashion. She wore couture clothing and fine jewelry. She shopped at stores like A & S, Ann Taylor, Lord & Taylor, Neiman Marcus, and Bergdorf Goodman. Prior to meeting Simi, I had never heard of these department stores.

She took me on one of her shopping sprees. She spent over two hundred dollars on a blouse. I almost fainted. Simi was the baby of her family. She had two older sisters. She was by her own admission, a spoiled kid. She was accustomed to getting what she wanted. She did not hesitate to call her mom to get an increase in her allowance. I thought that she was rich. She always had money. We always went out to dinner – her treat of course. I was always broke. My daddy could not send me money every time that I called home.

I was paying for my own college education by working. Simi's parents were paying her tuition. Simi's parents thought that working would interfere with her academic pursuits. They expected her to do well academically. They would not allow her to work. I understood their position.

Simi liked to party and shop. Class attendance was a low priority to her. In the end, she had to spend an extra semester in school in order to graduate. Eventually, Simi did get a job because her parents decided to cut off the funds that supported the "shopping" addiction.

I didn't know that Simi was developing other problems. Simi was always fashion conscious. Somewhere along the way, perhaps in her junior year, she decided to become more body conscious. She made a decision to go on a diet. She exercised multiple times during the day. The only drink that she consumed was a soft drink called Tab. She must have consumed about ten tabs per day. Her body was beginning to tone. The weight was slowing dissipating. She was looking good.

One day, Simi was in a fight with one of the girls who lived in our dorm. A dorm council hearing was held regarding the incident. Simi lost and consequently she was evicted from campus housing. I loved Simi, but she was always getting into trouble with the campus authorities.

Initially, she moved off campus into a rat infested (literally) efficiency apartment. This dump was not acceptable to Simi or her parents. I was still living in the dorms at the time. I hated dorm life. I felt like a prisoner. Simi approached me about the idea of sharing an apartment together and that's when we decided to move to Southeast D.C.

We had a lot of good times together in that apartment. We both had busy schedules. We were like ships passing in the night. One day, I took a good look at Simi's body. She looked sick. She had lost over 100 pounds. Her body was emaciated. I realized that she was sick, but I didn't know what was wrong with her. She said that she just needed to loose a few more pounds. I began to panic. At that moment, I realized that she was suffering from Anorexia Nervosa. Although I lived with her, I didn't see what she was doing to her body. The constant dieting, vomiting, and binge eating were all signs, that I didn't see until it was too late.

Simi graduated from college and return to New York. She began to get treatment for her disorder. At one point in time during her illness, she weighed 87 pounds! She was a walking skeleton. Her shiny skin had lost its luster. Her beautiful smile was gone. Her pearly white teeth looked out of place in the gauntness of her thin face. She looked pitiful. It hurt me to see her in such a state.

In 1983, she died in her sleep. She died in her childhood home in Freeport, New York. Anorexia had destroyed her heart muscle. She died from a heart attack. I didn't learn of her death until six months later. I made arrangements with her mother to visit her final resting place. In 1985, my first daughter was born. I named her Simone, in honor of my good friend, Simi.

STARVING SPIRITS

"No! I don't want to go to hell when I die. Please let me go to heaven. Please, Please, Please" I kept screaming. It was a dream, but it was so real. I woke up in a cold sweat. Have you ever had those dreams that are so vivid that they are terrifying? I was thirteen years old when I had a dream that I was doomed to live eternally in hell. I could see it. I could feel it. I was spiraling downward into hell. I couldn't stop.

When I awoke from the dream, I thanked God for waking me. What was the significant of that dream? My family lived in a double house in Piedmont. Our neighbors were Benny and his wife, Dorothy.

One of their sons, Earl, was a year older than me. Earl and I just could never get along. We fought and argued all the time. I don't remember why we argued. We both had strong personalities. I guess the synergy between the two of us simply brought out the negative side in both of our personalities.

In my dream, Earl and I were in some type of academic competition. In the dream, there was a man standing at the top of a mountain. This man was in charge of asking the questions. If you answered the question correctly, you went to heaven. If you answered it incorrectly, you went to hell.

You only had one chance to answer the question. You had to whisper the answer into the man's ear. So, no one got to hear the question or the answer. Once you answered the question, the man opened a door and you went through the door. You weren't seen again. We didn't know what was behind the door. Many people were standing in line to meet the man.

Earl and I were in line with the other "contestants" waiting for our turn. Finally, it was our turn to approach the man. Earl went up to the man. I saw the man whispered into Earl's ear. The door was opened and Earl vanished through the door. It was my turn next. I wasn't afraid of the man. I was afraid because I didn't know what was on the other side of the door.

I can't remember the question that he asked me. I could tell by the expression on his face that my response did not satisfy him. He told me to go to the left. As I enter through the doorway, I immediately slipped off of a steep cliff. Beneath me were roaring flames. Some of the previous contestants were swirling around just like me trying to stay out of the flames. It was as though we were suspended in animation.

When I looked above me, there was another dimension that looked cool, blue and beautiful. Earl was in that dimension traveling towards heaven. I was furious. I kept thinking to myself, I know that he did not give the right answer. How come he's going to heaven and I'm not? How could he get to go to heaven? It wasn't fair. I could see him moving gently and peaceably towards the heavenly clouds. I was spiraling downward into a consuming flame. Help! I kept screaming.

I woke up. The flames never touched me. However, they seemed so real. I knew that God was trying to send me a message through my dreams. What was God trying to tell me? I wasn't sure, but I needed to find out. I told my parents. They couldn't help me. I went to Sunday school on a regular basis. I thought that I was really a "good" girl. I didn't get into trouble. I studied and made good grades, so why was I going to hell.

Even at thirteen years old, I recognized that this dream was different from any others that I had ever had in my life. I couldn't stop thinking about that dream. It haunted me for weeks. Then one day, I was talking to my neighbor, Betty. I told her about the dream. She completely understood everything that I was describing to her. It was almost like she was there.

She told me that God communicates with all of us in many different ways. Perhaps the way to get my attention was through my dreams. My conversation with Betty changed my life forever. She assured me that the dream was not really about Earl and me. Instead it was about making the right choices in life. We all have the free will to choose right from wrong, good from bad or heaven or hell. We have to make choices. If we make the wrong ones, we have to pay the consequences. Sometimes there are no second chances.

It was no accident that I was thirteen when it happened. The dream probably would not have had such a profound effect upon my life if it had happened at any other time. Betty explained to me that life on earth is temporary. Our bodies are containers for our precious spirits. In order to preserve ourselves, we must feed our spirits. Our spirits must never starve. Nourishment for the spirit comes from searching for truth.

NASH RAMBLER

Paul, Stevie, Lynnie and I used to play house. Paul was my pretend husband. Lynnie was Stevie's "wife." Paul and I sat in the front seat of the Nash Rambler with our four children (my dolls). Lynnie and Stevie sat in the back seat with their children.

Our white doll babies were our children; we didn't have black dolls during that time period. Paul was always the driver of the car. Paul and Stevie would play house with us for a little while. When the other neighborhood boys wanted to play ball, Stevie and Paul immediately abandoned us.

My daddy had a 1958 Nash Rambler. He parked it in Grandma Laura's backyard next to the coal house. The car was always broken. It was never used as a vehicle. I used it as my playhouse.

Daddy would actually sleep in the car. He slept in the car, because sometimes my grandmother's house was overcrowded. There was no place in the house for my dad to sleep, He took blankets and quilts and slept in the car. I remember on more than one occasion, my grandmother sending me out from the comfort of her warm home into the back yard to check on my daddy and to wake him up so that he would not be late for work.

It's amazing what parents will do to keep their families together. The man that I admire the most in my life is my dad. He is hardworking, dedicated, honest and a fine example of a true father.

Both Paul and Stevie were my cousins. It would have been impossible for us to grow up and marry. Angie, Lynnie, Anita and I use to play all day long during the summer. Playing house in the Nash Rambler was just one of many activities. We did everything from "baking" mud pies to dancing in the streets to sounds of the Supremes and Stevie Wonder.

Although, we were poor, we had a great sense of community. Our lives were spontaneous and fun. We never had to worry about finding playmates. In an instant, one could find five or six kids to play ball, dolls, jacks or bingo.

We went from house to house making Kool-Aid Pops. We ate animal crackers. I still love animal crackers. We had our own carnivals, lemonade stands, and bake sales. Occasionally, Little Jim Coleman would give the kids in the neighborhood a ride on his motorcycle. Cousin Jake Redman would give us rides on his horse, Nugget.

During the summer months, all the neighborhood residents would and sit outside on their front stoops. You could hear the buzz of Mr. Otis' clippers. The tunes from the Gospel Harmonettes danced from the church windows only to clash with sounds of the Temptations. "My Cherie Amour" hummed from Faye Twyman's radio.

I remember those good old days on Paxton Street. I only wish that today's children could experience a community like Back Street, which consisted of two streets, Paxton and Water. I lived on both streets until I departed to go away to college in 1977.

Thea Garland – Girl Extraordinaire

Every neighborhood has a bully, goody two shoes, slow learner, nerd, fast girl, pretty boy, genius, druggie, church girl and of course, a tomboy. You probably remember all the folks in your neighborhood that fit one or more of these descriptions. Most neighborhoods have this diversity. Some communities deny this diversity. They attempt to hide their citizens who lived outside the norm. In our community, everyone was loved.

The tomboy was the girl in the community who could beat the boys, hated wearing dresses and despised frilly hairstyles. Often the tomboy possessed extraordinary athletic talent. The tomboy was a cute girl with ponytails and a lot of attitude. She rejected anything feminine.

Thea fit the description perfectly. She was a cute, honey browned skin girl with long ponytails and athletic build. She was our tomboy. Thea and I were cousins related on my Grandma Laura's side. Thea's Grandmother Ella Price Garland and my Great Grandmother Leila Price were sisters. Thea was about two years older than me. She was one of nine children born to Glendora and James Garland.

Thea's brother, Brian, and I were in the same class. Brian and I were good friends. Large African American families were very common in Piedmont. Most families in our neighborhood had an average of seven children. She was gifted both academically and physically. She could play just about any sport. She excelled in basketball and softball.

Thea had a great sense of humor. She made me laugh so hard that sometimes my stomach ached. We didn't play together very much because I was a "girly" girl. I loved playing with Barbie dolls. Thea would not have been caught dead playing with dolls.

Thea wouldn't play dolls with the "girly" girls. However, she would let us join her street teams. I admit that there are two talents that I am missing – musical and athletic. I must have been asleep when the Almighty was dispensing those gifts.

My most remarkable athletic adventure is walking. I have always had great motivational, organizational and leadership skills. Thea knew that I possessed these skills. I was the team cheerleader and organizer. I couldn't play the games, but I could get the kids organized. The Almighty gives each of us special talents. We can use our talents to work collaboratively on any project.

After school and during the summer months, our teams would meet at Roger Green's house; located near the end of Paxton Street. Roger and his siblings were all athletic. Roger was close to my age. He was a year a head of me in school. His sister, Eve, was my classmate. Roger was also our cousin. His Grandmother, Ethel Price Green, was the sister of my Great Grandmother, Leila Price and to Thea's Grandmother Ella Price Garland. We were all cousins.

Roger and Thea were always the team captains. I was always the last teammate chosen. No one wanted me on his or her team, because my skills were so bad. Although my skills were lacking, I still wanted to play. I couldn't pitch, bat, run or perform any of the necessary skills of the game.

Thea always felt sorry for me. She let me join her team. Roger would only select me if he were desperate. Captain Thea would put me up to bat first. Inevitably I would strike out. She knew that she would have to make up for my deficiency. That girl stole more bases than anyone on the team.

She was just good. She made extraordinary moves with her body. By the end of the game, she looked like she had been in a war. Her face was dirty. Her ponytails were dusty. She had scratches, cuts, and bruises all over body. She was happy because her team had won the game. She always went the extra mile for victory.

We played together everyday in our neighborhood. We knew one another's strengths and weaknesses. This was important as we entered into high school. I knew my limitations and so did Thea. I also knew that if I wanted to be on a winning intramural team – it had to be Thea's team. She realized that she would have to make up for my lack of athletic skill. I was the team leader when we played Jeopardy.

One year, Thea and I teamed up and won the table tennis championship. We received ribbons and trophies for our outstanding athletic accomplishments. I finally found a sport that I could master. Thea was patient with me. She taught me an important lesson. She taught me to have fun and to laugh at myself. She really was a serious and gifted athlete. She could compete with the best men and women in our community.

My youngest daughter, Alexis, reminds me of Thea. She is a tomboy and proud of it. Alexis says that the term tomboy is out of vogue. The appropriate term is simply athlete. Alexis began walking at eight months. She has been performing incredible feats with her body since then. She runs, swims, skates, plays basketball, baseball and climbs trees.

She is a daredevil. Did I mention that she doesn't play with dolls, wear dresses or put bows in her hair? Thea knows that Alexis definitely inherited her athletic DNA from her father, Lyle, and not her mother.

Paris

I don't know how many hours I spent baby sitting Brian and Wade. I spent many hours watching my cute charges. I had a baby-sitting business in order to save money to travel to France. Our High School French Club was planning a trip to Paris. I was extremely excited to travel to France. I had read many books about the history of France. I was also studying French. I thought that it was only appropriate that I actually visit France.

I approached our French teacher, Mrs. Mussen, about the idea of arranging a tour for the French Club to travel to France. She agreed to organize the trip and to help us with fundraising. It was a dream come true for me. The total cost of the trip was about six hundred dollars per person. We allowed ourselves one year to raise the money for the trip.

By 1975, we had moved into the middle class. Daddy had purchased us a home. He was making good wages at his job. He agreed to pay for half of my expenses for my trip. I would have to pay for the balance. We struck a deal. I would do whatever it took to get the money to go to Paris.

I had a babysitting gig just about every weekend. My primary clients were the two adorable sons of Fred and Cyl Taylor. It was fun watching them and Cyl and Fred paid very well. I saved every penny that I earned from babysitting for the trip. I can't believe that Brian and Wade are grown men now. At last count, Brian had four children.

My other charges were my niece and nephew, Shamona and Doug. I mostly got paid in kisses for watching them. I usually watched them for free. My sister knew that I was trying to raise money for the trip so she frequently paid me to watch her kids.

Throughout that year, we held bake sales, cider sales, candy sales, raffles, and calendar sales. We exceeded our fundraising goal. In March 1975 our group departed from Dulles International Airport for Paris. My friends, Jeanne and Todd went on the trip as well as Robin Washington, Linda Majors, and Ricky Bruce. There were some other students from nearby Ridgeley High School who also flew to Paris with us.

The Parisian sites were everything that I expected. I loved France. I felt at home because I had studied photographs of all the historic landmarks. I was very familiar with the history of those landmarks. I loved the Louvre, Notre Dame, the Champs Elysee, Eiffel Tower, Montmartre and the Seine.

We sailed on the Bateau Mouche down the Seine River, dined at the sidewalk Cafes, strolled along Rive Gauche (the left bank) and made fun of our tour guide, Pierre. Pierre had nicotine stained fingertips and a handlebar mustache. Todd and Jeanne said that he looked like a horror movie reject. We purchased scarves, perfume, patisseries, and wine to take home as souvenirs.

Our itinerary included a trip to the Loire Valley, which was wonderful. We toured the old world castles and the vineyards. We practiced the French Language. I must admit that classroom French and "real" French are two distinctively different experiences.

One evening we were taken to "La Cave," which was a real cave located outside of Paris. It had been transformed into a nightclub and restaurant. Ricky Bruce got just a little drunk and started flirting with the girls on the trip. The girls loved Ricky. The specialty of the house was Lapin (rabbit). I was adventuresome, so I tried the rabbit and it was delicious. You have to remember that I was accustomed to eating the wild and unusual concoctions prepared by my daddy.

I was fifteen years old when I visited France. I have visited other European countries since that time. I even spent a semester abroad in Italy when I was an undergraduate at American University.

I am confident that traveling is one of the best ways to get a good education. If I had my way, I would encourage everyone to take at least two years out of their lives just to travel to different places in the world. I remember when I first shared my dream of going to Paris with a few of my friends and family members.

They laughed at me because they thought that I was dreaming. They were partly right. I was dreaming, but I had faith that my dream would come true. I've always believed that if you can visualize your dreams you can make them come true. My trip to Paris was the first of many dreams that the Almighty fulfilled for me.

Miss Mabel's Custard

My maternal grandmother's name was Mabel Agnes Redman Gaiter. I got to know her best when we visited her and Granddaddy Pid during the summers. Granddaddy was a dark man with a strong physique. His body looked like it was made from steel. He was a willful man with a gentle touch for his grandchildren. Grandma was the antithesis of her husband. She was petite and dainty. Her skin was beautiful golden brown. She had gorgeous sky blue eyes.

You could tell that my grandparents loved one another just by the little things that they did together. They worked together in Grandma's small flower garden. They sat on the porch enjoying conversation. I loved to visit with them during for many reasons; perhaps the best reason was Grandma's cooking. I have been blessed in my life with two cookin' grandmothers and a cookin' mama. I think that those cookin' genes must have skipped me.

Every day was a culinary treat for us. Grandma's food was homemade. We never eat anything out of a can. The fruits and vegetables came from local farms or Grandma's garden. She baked her bread on a daily basis. We never ate store bought bread when we were at Grandma's house.

On Sunday, she would prepare golden fried chicken, mashed potatoes with gravy, slaw, green beans, rolls and iced tea. The beautiful flowers that adorned her table came from her flower garden. Like Grandma Mabel, I love fresh flowers. I try to always have a fresh floral arrangement on my dining room table as well as on my office desk. One of these days, I'm going to create my own home garden space and name it *Miss Mabel's Flowers* in honor of my grandmother.

Grandma's recipes were committed to her memory. Only she knew the secret of her cooking masterpieces. She never used any modern conveniences. For many years she relied upon her cast iron stove for cooking. Have you ever seen a cast iron stove? I have and believe me, it's not an easy task working with wood and fire to cook a meal. Women today cannot complain, with all the modern conveniences that we have in our kitchens. We have all these gadgets and we still can't cook like our mothers.

One of my favorite treats that Grandma used to make was custard. She generally made the custard during the Christmas Holidays. It was scrumptious and it tasted even better when it was drizzled over her homemade cake. One regret that I have in life is that I don't have that custard recipe. I would love to taste that custard again.

Granddaddy passed away when I was thirteen years old. It was so difficult to bear when he passed away. I loved him so much. He was the quintessential grandfather. He didn't have much financial wealth, but he gave us much love. He used to bounce me on his knee, tickle me and give me kisses.

Grandma lived for almost thirty years after Granddaddy's transition. She outlived all of her children, except for my mother, Suellen. She departed this life when she was close to 100 years old. We actually thought that she was 102 when she died.

When she passed away, her brown skin was without wrinkles. She was still petite. I can envision Solomon and Mable sitting on a porch in heaven reminiscing about the good days in Petersburg, West Virginia.

NINK

My grandmothers adorned their etageres with pictures of their children, grandchildren and great grandchildren. The photographs of my uncles dressed in their military uniforms especially intrigued me. My grandfathers, uncles, cousins, nephews and brother have all served in the armed forces.

I don't really remember the Vietnam War that well. However, I do recall the protest songs and the sadness that the war brought to our community. Some of the men that left our Piedmont community never returned. Those who did return were physically and psychologically changed for life. Many of the Vietnam Vets in our town became drug addicts. I can't imagine what images of war can do to the psyche of an individual.

The most poignant memory, that I have about the war, involved my cousin Nink. My cousin, Lawrence "Nink" Redman came to live with us because of severe injuries that he had sustained in the war. Nink was my first cousin on my mother's side of the family. His mother, Ardella or "Aunt Sis," as we called her, died when Nink was a young man. Aunt Sis passed away when I was about four years old. She was the mother of Wayne, Willie Joseph "Joker," Nink, Theresa, Gordy and Fred.

My mother served as a surrogate mother to her late sister's children. When Nink became injured, it was only logical that he would come to our home to recover. He was severely burned on the back of his body. His neck, back and lower torso were raw and pink from the burns. We took turns helping him to properly cleanse and medicate his back. Mom had to constantly sanitize the sheets on his bed to prevent any infection from occurring.

As his wounds started to heal they began to itch. He would cry in pain and agony. It didn't help that it was summer time. We didn't have any air conditioning in our home. I don't think that anyone in our neighborhood had air conditioning. Summers are not like they used to be.

During my childhood years, the weather got very hot. It was hell on earth for Nink. It hurt all of us to witness his pain. It was a terrible time for him and it took many years and skin grafts for his recovery. He managed to survive his ordeal. He lived with us for several months. I felt sorry for him every day.

After he recuperated, he relocated to Philadelphia and started a new life. In 1994 he passed away. I would like to think that he is sitting on that porch in heaven with his mother Ardella and Grandma and Granddaddy. I will always remember him as a noble veteran.

THE MAJESTIC THEATRE

In Piedmont, we had our own movie theatre. It was only open on the weekend. Mr. Welch from Westernport, the neighboring town, and his wife owned and operated the theatre. The theatre was used as a movie house and quasi dance center.

The space between the screen and the seats was large enough for 10 to 15 kids to dance. Mr. Welch allowed us to dance before the weekly feature was shown. The favorite song of the day was "Wipe Out." We danced to many Beatle songs and Motown Sounds.

Every time I hear Wipe Out song, I think of Sue Ann Spiker. She was a teenager. Her physique was skinny. She had short blond hair. She came to the Majestic every week because she liked to dance. My friend, Rochelle Kithcart, always said that Sue Ann needed to sit her bony butt down because she didn't have any rhythm and definitely couldn't dance. Despite Chelle's criticism, Sue Ann continued to shake her skinny torso to the beat of Wipe Out.

Our movie selections included Beach Blanket Bingo, Help, Yellow Submarine, Elvis Presley, or a scary movie. That was it! Occasionally, we would get a current movie. One special showing was the movie "A Patch of Blue" starring Sidney Poitier. That was one of my favorite movies. In reality we didn't go to the theatre to watch the movie, we went there to play and chase one another.

White girls and some black girls were in love with Rick Butler. He was our community's teen heartthrob. Sue Ann Spiker was his main flame. You could usually find them in a corner kissing. As a matter of fact, there were a lot of teens kissing in the Majestic. I guess it was Piedmont's little love hangout.

You couldn't get into too much trouble in the Majestic because Mr. Welch would come around with his long, bright flashlight and check on us. If you were misbehaving, he would not hesitate to send you home. I believe that Mr. Welch probably knew all of our parents. We knew that we better be on our best behavior.

One summer evening, I decided to go to the Majestic. I knew all the regulars, but this particular night there was a new boy in town. He was the cutest boy that I ever seen. He was light complexioned with "good" hair. He was a little taller than me. I think that he was about my same age. He was sitting with the girls from up on the hill.

I sent my spy, Lynnie (Chelle's sister), to get some information about the cute boy. When she returned she had a full report to give to me. She whispered into my ear "The boy's name is Randy Gilmore. He is visiting Lenora and Ruby. His dad and Ruby's mom are dating. He's from Ohio," I had all the information that I needed. My next move was to become friendlier with my cousins, Ruby and Lenora, to get to more information about Randy.

Ruby and Lenora were my cousins on my Grandmother Laura's side of the family. Their mother, James (yes, James), and my grandmother were first cousins. They were raised as sisters. I was in luck, or so I thought. When the time was right, I approached Lenora and got the 411 on Randy. I was disappointed to learn that he liked some other girl. Naturally, he wouldn't disclose the identity of the girl. All I knew was that he didn't like me. This was my first heartbreak.

After the movies were over, I went home and sat on my porch. I told my mom that I had seen a cute boy at the movies. I told her that I liked him. I told her his name and in a deep breath she said, "Oh no, Gayedy, you can't like him. He's your cousin! That's Buck Gilmore's boy. We're related to them on my daddy's side of the family." I couldn't win. Even if Randy wanted me to be his girlfriend, the elders in the family would have forbid such a relationship.

It amazed me that someone who I had never met was instantly my cousin. I accepted the fact that I was related to everyone in the universe. I guess you can say that knowing your family roots is important.

I knew that in order to make a successful love hook up; I would have to avoid any guy with the who had the last name Price, Redman, Gilmore, Washington, Gaiter, Clay, Spillard, Smith or Richards. There is definitely value in knowing your family tree. I learned that lesson at an early age.

Tell your family's stories! The future generations need to know about their ancestors.

My parents- Suellen Gaiter Clay and Russell Clifton Clay

Photo credit: Alexis C. Peck

Leontyne Clay Peck
leontynepeck@gmail.com

The author of **"Our Mother's Dresses: An Ancestry Tribute to my African, European and American Mothers," "Silver Children: The African American Family of Henry Clay," and "Paxton Street"**

Her books can be purchased directly from her or through Lulu Publishing or from other outlets such as Amazon.

She is married to Lyle Peck and they are the parents of two adult daughters, Whitney and Alexis.